I0474977

AZaz
Stand Up and Stand Out

From Team Leader to CEO

By Bryan L. Hartson, Sr.

Third Edition 2023

For my beautiful wife of 16 years Patricia, Bryan Jr. – my 4 year old son and best friend, Kaitlynn and Ashley, my two beautiful daughters, the heart of why I get up each day. I'd like to recognize all that have reported to me and followed my lead, taken the leap and made the teams that changed the lives of thousands.

Kisses good morning and Kisses good night.

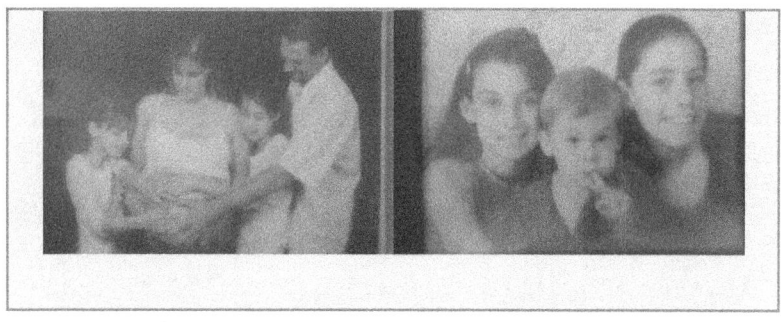

In Memory of my mother, Beverly Patricia Hartson

Contents

Forward

This is a book for the leader that wants to move to the next level. It's not top down management, it's critical thinking. I've spent a lot of time with poor management and a lot of time with great management. I believe the points in this book are critical and missed in many leaders. One of my favorite sayings is, "You don't have to like me, but you will respect me". In this book I hope to show you some low hanging fruit on how to get your team to respect you from any level of management no matter how small or how big the company.

This short book was created to address the beginner or the seasoned person not sure of the new way. I have spent time with business professional leadership instructors and have changed their way of traditional thinking. This book holds the secrets to great leadership. There are many many additional tools I can teach but these are the low hanging fruit that I believe will take you to the next level. In some cases, it is what you know and, in some cases, it's who you know. I address both.

The most important thing to know is to know your processes and your teams from the top down, regardless of your level of management. If you own the company, you must spend time with all levels, including the front line. This is your face to the world. While this is a guide based on life experiences, character names have been altered.

There are many things that a good Team Leader, Manager, Sr. Manager, Director, AVP, VP, etc. do on a day to day basis. Things such as run reports, analyze reports, and give updates to the executive team and board of directors; look at processes; justify performance. One thing that is overlooked is the morale on the floor and the personal interaction with the division and company.

In reality, the closer you are to the front line, the more time you need to spend with your associates. Team Leaders should spend 75 percent of their time with their associates and they should be on the floor. Answer the complaint call. It's good customer service! The percentages reverse as you go up levels, but even the President and CEO should spend 15% of their time on the floor.

You know, one of the shows I LOVE to watch is Undercover Boss. Just love the show. What gets me though, every week, is when the CEO goes undercover and discovers so many different things, like who works well, what is working well, who has great ideas, and then they are always amazed at what the discover isn't working. Every time I say out loud to the T.V. (like that CEO can hear me) "Isn't that Management 101?!"

Being a great leader means that you can get things done. That's the Manager part of management. Getting your staff to love and follow you is the leader part of management. Here's some visual signs you're doing the right thing.

♥ Bryan aka (Boss!) ♥
thank you for all of your
mentoring! You are truly so much
fun to work with and for ♡
We appreciate you and all your
hard work! You Rock!!!
                    xoxo
                        Natalie C.

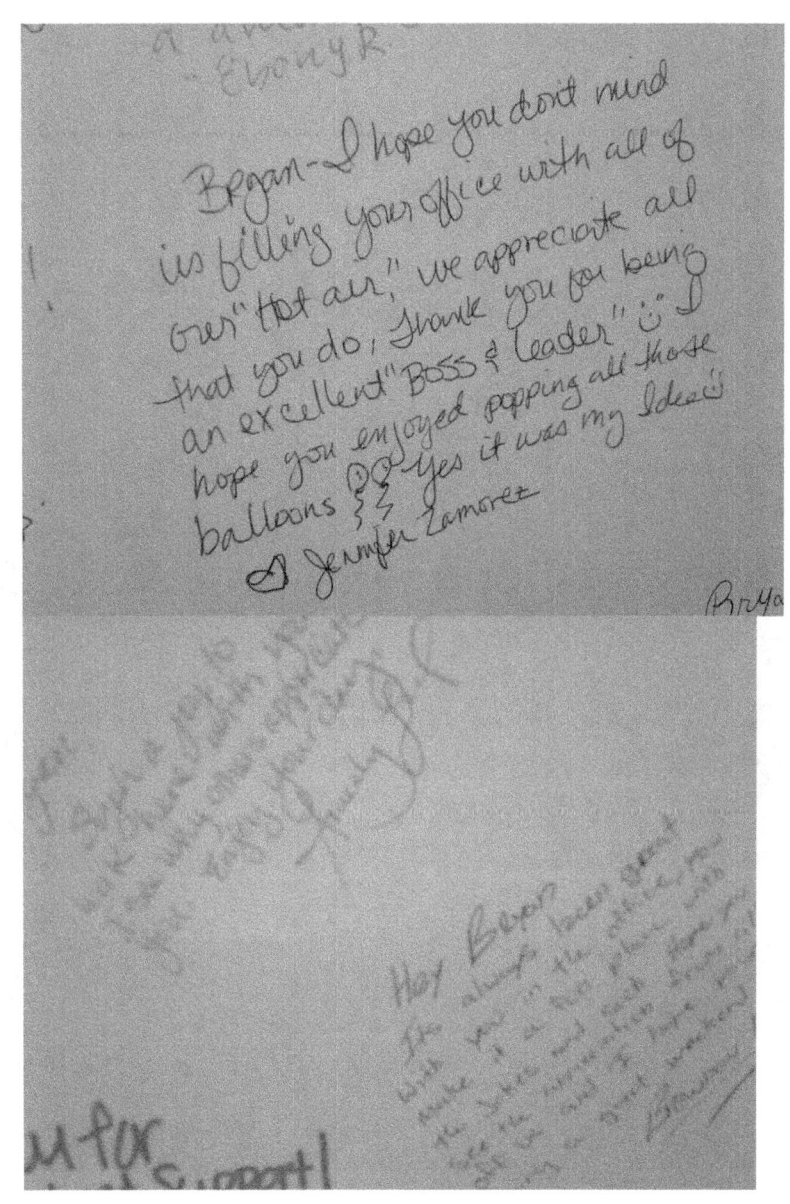

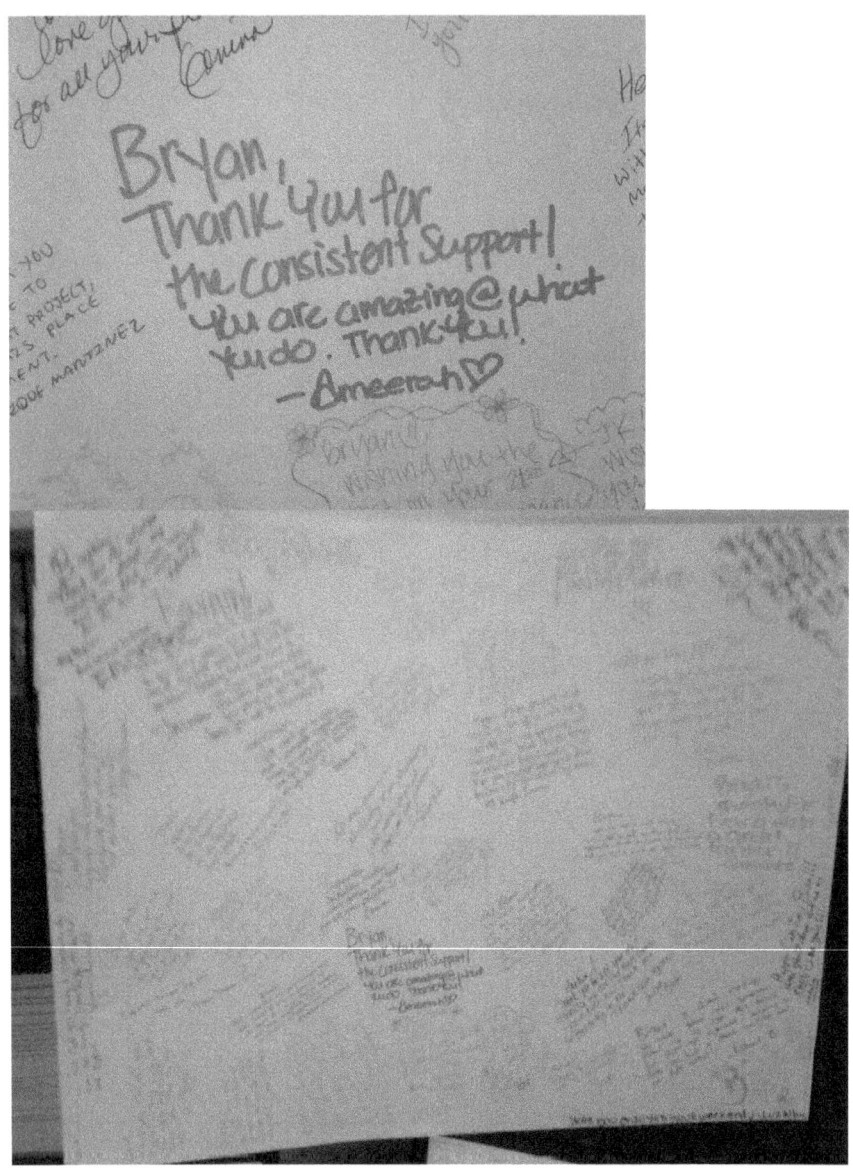

One must build a strong foundation with other Divisions, lead their division and make persuasive arguments. Not an easy thing to do. Let's take a quick look at how Adriana and Jessie handle their teams when, in a call center, the number of calls holding jump up. Keep in mind that Jessie is not in the office. Adriana is manning the shop!

The Bad – Good Associate

Adriana recognizes that the calls are increasing in the queue so, as instructed by her boss, she jumps up and yells across the floor, "Everyone needs to get on inbound! Calls are backing up!". Adriana goes back to reading her emails and analyzing her quality reports on her staff that just came in.

Five minutes pass and Adriana realizes that three agents are not logged in to inbound. They are in a 'not ready' state. Adriana immediately sends and email to Jessie which says:

> "Jessie,
> Today we had 5 calls in queue for 5 minutes and I instructed everyone to go to inbound. Again, 3 people on your team –MaLisa, Jan and Jezebel were in not ready. This is getting old. I think you should do something about it."

Adriana sends a screen shot of the queues to Jessie as well.

Fast forward one day. Jessie arrives for work. Immediately, Jezebel says, "um Jessie, I don't know what happened yesterday, but I might have done the wrong thing. I didn't go on inbound while calls were holding, and I heard from across the room Adriana say calls were holding but I was reacting to your email that said to hit our deadline and not go inbound unless another manager sends an email to the group distribution email. That way we'll know it is being directed to us to go inbound."

Jessie was understanding, "So you did what you were told but are afraid you did the wrong thing? No worries. Next time a manager tells you to do something, just either explain why you aren't on board with doing it because I've given you direction to do something else or make the call to do it. Adriana will tell you if she wants to override me. That's fine. You get your direction from the person in authority and if Adriana and I need to have an offline, we can debrief and prepare for next time. It's important you are all getting a clear message on what to do. I'll circle back to Adriana later and see where the breakdown occurred."

Jessie is called in to his boss' office, Larry. Larry says, "Jessie, we need to have a talk. Three of your people didn't do what they were told. I was told that yesterday we had calls in queue and apparently an email was sent to the group to go inbound, and they refused to log in. I know you've already given them clear direction on what to do, but this is the second time in as many weeks that Adriana has told me they are not reacting quick enough. Have another talk with them. If it happens again, I think it's time to write them up. I mean, if Adriana is giving them direction, don't you think they should listen to her and act immediately? After all, she IS a manager."

Jessie replies back, "Absolutely. I'll get right on it. If they do it again, I'll fire them."

Larry replies, "Well I don't know if I'd go THAT far but they need to do what a manager tells them to do."

Jessie says, "I know, Larry. I got an email from Adriana last night that the ladies were told to go inbound and they didn't. I spoke with them this

morning and here's what happened. They were instructed by me that they needed to meet their deadline on contacting the fallout clients by end of day tomorrow and to do that they needed to stay on outbound unless instructed otherwise by me or a manager by email to go inbound. You and Adriana were on that distribution list."
Larry replies, "Ah, yes. I did see that."

Jessie continues, "There was no email sent. Adriana spoke across the room for everyone to go inbound. I spoke with MaLisa, and she stated that she was on break and didn't know about anything, Jan had to go in not ready or she would violate going over her 5 hours before lunch violation rule and Jezebel, the leader of the group, didn't know if she should follow my direction or go inbound. I had a talk with Jezebel and told her that if a manager makes a request to do something she must either do what she is told, challenge the request to the manager asking what she should do and why she isn't addressing the rising call volume or explain why she is not doing what is requested. There was no email which is where the confusion lay with her. She understands. This is her first time leading a group and I want to give her a little latitude. She's really doing a good job."

Larry commented, "Yes, she is. She's really stepped up. And as usual, Jessie, you are ahead of me on this. Good job!"

Jessie then circles back to Adriana. "Adriana, got a second? I just got through talking to Larry about my team and the email you sent me yesterday on them not going on inbound. Did you talk to them? "Adriana says, "No, I said it across the floor that everyone needed to go inbound. I don't know why they don't listen!"

Jessie replied, "It might be a good idea if you did next time. As I told Larry, one was at break, one was getting ready to go to lunch and approaching her fifth hour and the third didn't know what to do. Not sure if you recall, but I sent an email out the specialty group advising them not to go outbound at all unless they got an email to the distribution group stating to go inbound. I put all the managers on it and Larry. I talked to you about it yesterday too."

Adriana comments, "Ohhh, that's right. Forgot about that one. Just saw the calls in queue and freaked out for a minute."

Jessie replied, "No worries. Would you mind just touching base with them next time? I asked them to seek clarification out next time too. Would have avoided this getting to Larry. Remember we agreed to give Jez a team to lead, and we need to give her a little latitude to do it and make some mistakes. Our KPI's (Key Performance Indicators) are well within limits and even if we blew up a bit, we'd hit target. We need to let Jez slip a bit so she can grow, and while she has a safety net. She has to be allowed to make mistakes. When I'm done developing her and that safety net is gone, it's a whole different story."

Adriana finishes, "I can do that. Sorry."

What is the lesson in this situation?

You can never jump to a conclusion. Get your facts down. Your peers will generally assume that your workers are not working on purpose. That is not generally the case if you have good workers…your stars. When you are a 'star' however, all the focus is on you and everything you do wrong (so it's important to check and double check your data before publishing it – side note).

Jezebel was talked to by Jessie and it was explained that when a manager says to do something, do it. Explain why you are not doing it or seek advice. Simple. Free coaching (I Love free coaching's).

Don't overreact! If you are caught off guard, accept the feedback and let your boss know you'll look in to it and get back to him or her. It's easy to jump off the deep end and assume. It's better to take the information in, process it, investigate as deeply as you need to, give guidance and circle back with the findings to your boss. All will appreciate this MUCH more.

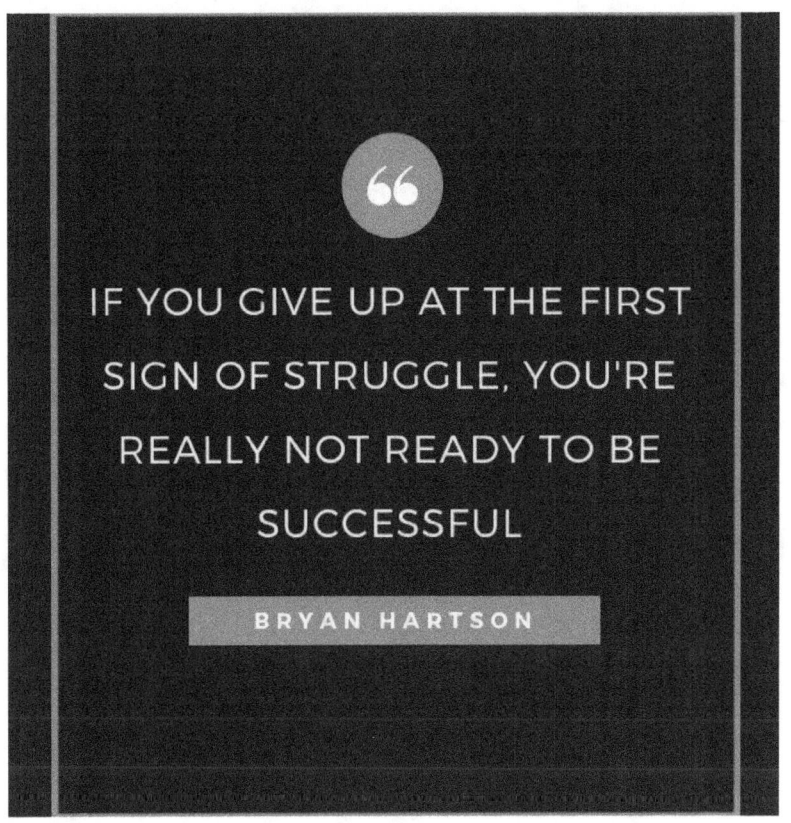

IF YOU GIVE UP AT THE FIRST SIGN OF STRUGGLE, YOU'RE REALLY NOT READY TO BE SUCCESSFUL

BRYAN HARTSON

> *Get in front of it.*

Teach your team to get you up to speed quickly on issues before they become an issue.

Because Jezebel approached Jessie as soon as she saw him, Jessie was able to get in front of what she anticipated would happen – the situation being escalated.

Jessie was able to get his facts down in advance. I believe it is always important to set the expectation for your team that your team can bring things to you that they are not happy with or are struggling with. I like to have the conversation, "I believe in skip levels. This is where you get in a room with my boss, without me. You discuss whatever you'd like. The only thing I'd like to ask is that if there is ever anything that you would tell my boss that isn't working or where I need improvement, I ask that you give me the opportunity to address it with you first. Get me in front of it. I will either explain why it is what it is, look at getting it fixed or explain why it can't be fixed now. Your opinion does count. Remember, doesn't mean it will be your way, but one change out of 5 ideas is a pretty good record to have and it shows all that you are not just a complainer but a fixer."

Finally, tie the loose ends up. Jessie went to Adriana and politely let Adriana know she escalated something that didn't need to be

STAND UP AND STAND OUT

escalated and recapped what they had agreed to the day prior. Jessie had his ducks in a row. Make sure you fight for your associates when fighting is warranted (I don't mean literally fighting or yelling, I mean persuasive guidance and discussion).

I remember when I came on board to a company that had part employees and part temp employees. Temp employees were not hired on to full time employees. One day I put together an argument on one of my Temp employees. It was specific and tangible and gave very specific reasons why this temp should be hired as a permanent employee. I asked for a few minutes of time with the Sr. VP. and gave my presentation. Less than 5 minutes later, he said, "O.k., process the paperwork and I'll approve it."

When word got out that this person was permanent, one manager came to me and said, "Bryan, I know you are well known and liked around here but I don't think it's fair that [insert employee name here] was hired permanent. I have people that I want hired and have asked several times but the answer has always been NO!".

I asked how he presented the request and he said that he asked. I asked what tangibles did he present and this manager didn't understand what I was saying. When I presented to this manager the tangibles that I had given, he looked puzzled and said, "I didn't do that. That's a really good idea." He went on to say, "I've been watching you and I have a lot to learn. Would you mind mentoring me?"

Of course, I am a huge fan of mentoring and agreed as long as he took his lessons and used them. You see, not all great performers are leaders. You need to find the diamond in the rough and structure it.

Good-Old School

There's a way to manage a division the right way, even when your peers are of an old school mentality that their way is the best way. Implement 'this' change...because I said so and it's the best fix.

Wrong.

If you want a successful business, change. Get input. Think. Do the job yourself.

One can learn a lot from doing the job themselves. I like to get myself on the floor once a month and do the job that the agents do. Why? It's simple. #1, you find out how hard their job is to cover every base and get 100% on quality. #2, it gives you a sense of what needs to be changed to make the division work smother. #3, the associates love it. They love than you are trying to do their work, they love that you care, they love that you have faults, and they love that they might be able to beat you at some task – maybe the number of

Check by phones they can get in an hour vs. you! This is HUGE with the staff.

The day of "this is the way it is because I said so" *should be over. We should continually be keeping ourselves in check with reality and the changing world. We really do not have all the best ideas. They come from the floor (the workers). Who does the work? Not you – If you think this is the case, who died and made you boss? Oh, wait, your boss did. O.k., so take responsibility and a stand. You should make a clear case why things need to change and how. Get it from your team. Challenge your peers. Stand Up and Stand Out!.*

Now, with that said, don't think that I am saying that everything your team tells you is the right way. You need to use your brain. Think. That's what you are really paid to do. The message should be along the lines of 'Your opinion counts. It doesn't mean I am going to use it, but it counts.'

This sends a message that your associates (and I call them associates instead of employees because they are a part of the growing business vision if you do it correctly) are able to make the company grow and their voice is heard. So many good ideas come from listening to associates on the front line and holding skip level meetings (where you meet with a team without the Supervisor present) and an open-door policy that truly is an open door!

I had someone tell me once "Why don't we have a beach theme day". Never would happen in the company because it was strictly dress professional M-F and Jeans on Saturday. I listened and found it to be a compelling idea. I Ran it up the ladder with clear reasons why it would be a great idea and boom....approved. The result was very positive for the division. They had fun. It was a result of one person being able to suggest.

I've had a ton of great ideas generated from the Division staff. I've implemented many. The key is to give credit where credit is due. They weren't my ideas, rather the ideas of my staff or my staff's staff or my staff's staff's staff...You get the picture. I am only as good as my associates. This is a statement that every leader should learn. I have taken awards and in each given my speech that I repeat throughout the years. "Thank you for this honor. This is truly a great accomplishment. This award goes to everyone who reports into me directly or indirectly. Your work is my success or failure and is my report card on my performance. Thank you for making ME look good."

Get Yourself Out There

Several years ago, I started a job I knew nothing about. I started at the bottom but before I started, I was told I was overqualified for the entry level position. I called the boss of the Division and said…but…but…but…

The Manager at the time was nice enough to let me join the team after he agreed to meet with me in his office. I explained myself to him and I remember him leaning back in his nice chair and then saying, "You are way overqualified for an entry level job and I don't have any Team Leader or Supervisor spots open." I gave him my commitment to the company and, well, that was that. He said he'd put me on the fast track to management (which didn't happen under his watch). I sat in a cubicle and learned how to collect on delinquent loans.

I was a busy worker and was promoted twice within a 3-month period of time to a harder collection portfolio. For some reason I caught the eye of the Vice President of the Division, we'll call him Jeff, who put me through the "University" he had created. This University was where he would spend a couple hours every other week in a class setting of me and a very small handful of other people and teach us the ropes in things from managing people to dealing with HR issues to strategies and techniques. This was much different than the "Top-Down" management style I had developed working for other companies. Including the University, I was previously the Executive Officer of. It was a wealth of information I still use today, but that's another book. Remember Jeff because I will circle back to him a bit later.

I always gave it my all and over the next several months the company grew and grew and grew. Team Leaders were added, Supervisors were added and Managers were added. It grew to over 85 billion dollars in product.

I interviewed 13 times, I believe, for the Team Leader spot. The interviews were conducted by Team Leaders and Managers. If you made it by the Team Leaders, you got to a manager. 13 times I made it to the Managers. 13 times I *didn't get the spot. The questions in the interview where standard questions such as, tell me about yourself, what are your strengths and weaknesses, you have an impressive resume, why do you want this job and the like.*

I was never asked if I wanted feedback, but I always asked what I could focus on. 13 times the response was, "You know, Bryan, it was really close. It was between you and so and so. There is nothing really to change. Keep doing what you're doing." One time a leader position was filled and the next day that same leader was fired. Guess who got the spot next...Not me. Later, one of my better leaders and mentor told me the reason. The other leaders knew that if I joined the team, they'd have to WORK...Amazing!

After about 9 months with the company the Manager was no longer working there and was replaced by a female as Sr. Manager. I learned a lot. Good and bad. She was very aggressive, associate oriented and very talented. Quickly, she recognized my talent and took me under her wing. As time went on over the years, my reputation grew and I had the pleasure of being mentored by her, by the person that replaced her and by the president of the company. It doesn't get any better than that.

Back to the beginning…Every day I would spend a couple hours with her, the new Sr. Manager, in her office behind closed doors for development.   Every   day   I   learned something…I quickly also learned that I'd have a new task to perform every time I went in to her office! After about two months of this, she called the Team Leaders, Supervisors and Managers in to a conference room…Oh, and she also called me in to the meeting as well.

She started off the meeting by saying, "Today, someone in this room is getting promoted!" Previously, promotions were pretty much by tenure and not by accomplishments. She went on… "This person became the first person to create and expand a brand new department, has written the policies and procedures for the department, has taken escalated calls and Executive complaint calls, is on the Executive Task force Team…" The list went on for a few minutes with specific achievements I had made.

As each accomplishment was announced more and more leaders in the room looked back at me. The questions came one by one. "Bryan, is it you?" And by the time she was ready to make the announcement that I was the next Team Leader, the best thing happened. Leaders were now saying, "Bryan, it IS you!"

There was a lot of whispering about how unfair it was that I got the promotion. There was even more whispering just 3 months later when she pulled everyone in to a room and said, "Today, someone in the room is being promoted to Supervisor" and began listing the accomplishments of this Team Leader. It was me.

Three or four months later when she pulled everyone in to a room again, the old school mentality was gone, leaders had left, on their own or not and she started up again..." Today, someone in this room is being promoted" again going on to list many of the accomplishments I had accomplished. I was now one of the Managers. The Supervisor I first reported to was now a manager, we will call her <u>Kim</u> (and I'll circle back to her in a bit too), an outside

Manager was hired and the two managers that were there…were no longer there…along with several of the old school Supervisors and Team Leaders. The associates were now engaged, productivity was up and there was very good structure in place, with a lot of improvement still needed. Oh, and that Sr. Manager that took me under her wing. She was now the Vice President of the Division.

Not too long after this, there was a re structure of titles and positions. The Sr. Manager position was eliminated from the company. I knew my boss was going to be around for a while so the possibility of me taking that spot was slim to none for a while and besides, I liked all the development I received. It really didn't matter much to me because I continued to receive healthy increases in pay, continued development and I had a great relationship with many of the Executive team, including the person who would later become President. Even the CEO to this day is a part of my professional networking source online.

Just so happens that about a year or so later, they re opened the Sr. Manager position. I was *the first to get it. The next Sr. Manager position was opened in another division about ½ a year later and a lady that was a pervious peer of mine for quite a while ended up getting it. Well deserved too.*

I remember a time when the Sr. Vice President came to my office and said, "Bryan, I don't know if we are going to meet our goal this month. I'm a little worried." I let her know of the strategies I was changing and said, "Have I ever told you we would hit our goal and not been right?" She replied with a no and said, "I'll tell you what Bryan. If we don't go up, I'll take you to Vegas."

On the first of the month, I ran my numbers at about 3 a.m. and when I got in the office at 8 a.m., there was the Sr. V.P. She asked, "So, do you think we did it?!" I said, "Yep. I ran the numbers. You'll see when the official numbers come out from the official source."

When they did, she was the first one in my office. "Bryan! You were right! I need to go tell [The president]. No, No. You do it! Here" and handed me the official report.

I walked over to the President's office, and she was on the phone with her door closed. As I started to leave, she opened the door and said, "What is it?" I gave her the report and shook my head. "You'll have to see for yourself. Sorry." I spoke. She asked, "That bad, hu?"

She took the report and read it. Then she looked at me in shock and started jumping up and down. She gave me a great big hug and gave me her gratitude.

I reminded her it wasn't because of me, it was because of my Division's hard efforts and strategic changes throughout the month. She still said, "I know, but you're the one that led them there and made it happen."

The Sr. V.P. did end up taking me to Vegas. As a matter of fact the whole Sr. Management team! It was a good time. It was a working vacation, but we had our fun too.

And Then There Were Rules!

I don't know if you are a big fan of NCIS, but I am. For years, I have often been nicknamed "Gibbs". Gibbs has rules. So do I.

Rule #1: Get the Right Person

Interview your candidates well. Ask situational questions, not general data heavy questions. I'll show you a good example in a minute. Ask follow up questions. Look at the timeline from when the person is pulling from. Is it years ago or is it recent? Are there specific details? Is the answer long winded? Is it specific? If it was a performance question that was lacking, what steps were taken to fix it? If the interviewee could go back and change anything, what would it be?

Write down their answers, but start the interview with, "John, in 30 seconds or less, tell me about yourself." See if they stick to the 30ish seconds and give you substantial information. By the way, I don't rely on resumes for an interview. They are nice to have and I review them for punctuation errors, grammar, gaps in employment history, job hopping...but that's about all.

Next let the person know what is going to happen in the interview. If you do it right, it will be like none they have ever had before! "John, I'm going to ask you some situational based questions. What I am looking for is to have you give me a detailed and specific instance that you have faced in the situation. It doesn't have to be in your current job, it can be in a past job or personal life. I'm going to be taking some notes, so I may not have eye contact with you, but I am listening, o.k.?" This sets the tone.

After the interviews are all done, put your papers together. Go to a white board and write the strengths of your team on the white board and their weaknesses. Now pull out your candidates and write their strengths and weaknesses on the white board. Where the candidate that fills the biggest weaknesses in your team is, this is the candidate you want. You do not want a bunch of mini you's.

What is a situational question? Here's a couple to think about. They're hard to admit to sometimes.

For a Leader or higher position, ask questions such as:

- ➢ *Tell me a time when you witnessed someone doing something unethical.*

- ➢ *Tell me a time when you had a deadline to meet and you knew you weren't going to make it.*

- ➢ *Tell me a time when morale on your floor was down. What did you do?*

- ➢ *Tell me a time when you had someone working for you that was not performing. This is a good one. You want swift action. Look at the timeline for what they did to coach the person up or out. Usually, your first answer will be one of a success story for the person. Follow up with, "Great. That's fantastic that you were able to turn the person around.*

- ➢ *Now, tell me of a time when it didn't work out and you had to let the person go." This one is important. You never want a Manager or higher to say anything like,*

"I've never had to do that." This person either didn't hold the power in the position to do it, pawned it off on someone else or didn't manage their direct reports very well to their standards (generally). You have many more questions to ask if this is the case.

Here's' a great question that is not situation based but thought process based and can turn in to a situational based question. "If you had a deadline that had to be met, but in meeting it, you would jeopardize the morale of your floor, which would you choose? The morale or the deadline?" Follow it up with, "Give me an example where this happened to you." There's not a right or wrong answer, just an answer. Usually you'll get what they think you, the boss, want to hear. "Well, definitely the deadline…"

A good answer is, "It depends. If the deadline was moveable or not significant, I'd move the deadline. If the deadline was not movable, I'd have to sacrifice the morale. To do this I would communicate to all that the missed deadline would impact and ask them to understand that we will target the deadline for completion. I'd communicate to the staff that had to meet the deadline that it is not moveable and ask for their support.

I do a lot of things for my teams like adjust schedules to allow other things in their life to take place, reward performance, etc. I'd ask them to bend for me on this one."

Follow Up Points

➢ *Let them talk. Not too long but let them talk. It will tell you a lot about their style, their attention to detail, etc. Observe what kind of a story they are telling you. You may want a someone who is long winded on your team. You may want someone who is descriptive in their details on your team. Depends on what weakness you are trying to fill in the team. The interview process is the first line in picking the right person. It's not just about the questions, but the answers given, body language, words used. Observe everything.*

➢ *Ask follow up questions when they give you an answer. The first two questions or so that you ask, they will most likely tell you a general story without being specific. It's o.k. to interrupt and say, "Thank you for that, John, what I am really looking for is a specific instance you encountered. Tell me about a specific instance and what happened." If they can't think of anything, then move on. Note this though because this could be an issue of failing to confront. If they did nothing about the ethical issue, that's o.k. Ask what they would do different. They'll usually say something like, "I guess I should have told my boss, their boss, H.R.," whatever! That's o.k. That means they may be coachable.*

➢ *Ask follow up questions such as 'what did you do about it', 'how did that make you feel', 'what did you do next', and 'how did that make you feel'.*

➢ *Watch their actions speech patterns, tone of voice. Make sure you look for characteristics for your specific shop. If it's a call center, close your eyes for a second. How does the person sound? This is the only thing the customer will see…or in this case, hear…is their voice. If it is sales, how does the person sound? Dress? Did they comb their hair? Did they make eye contact with you? How firm was their shake when they first shook your hand?*

➢ *If you are interviewing for a leader, you want to ask question specific to that position. If it's a Team Leader, you want to ask about leading a group of 10-15 people questions and the specific job functions for that position. If it's a Supervisor position, ask questions about leading a group of 5-8 Leaders. If it's a Manager position you want to ask questions around leading 5-7 Supervisors...and so on and so on.*

➢ *Once a determination is reached on who is getting the position, it is very appropriate to offer feedback to the candidates that did not get the position(s). My preference is to send an email to the candidates and inform them of the fact that the position has been filled. I also like to add the piece, "If you'd like feedback on your interview, please let me know and I will schedule some time with you to discuss." This leaves the door open to the person who wants to improve. I will not seek the candidates out to give them feedback.*

➢ *Your feedback should be specific and tangible to what you found in the interview that made the candidate not the choice for you. Feedback should NEVER be general in nature.*

Know Your Team

One of the most important things to a successful division is a leader who leads and knows their team. When you take on a new team or member of a team, it is important to set expectations from day #1. The expectations should be set for what you expect from the team and what they can expect from you. Getting their input on anything else they expect from you is excellent. This will give you a pulse of who needs what. Some need constant attention and others would rather be to themselves. Each member of your team needs to be lead differently. Get to know your team. Document your coaching and meetings. For meetings, I usually have one of the team take notes and I usually let different people present things in meetings. It gets them involved.

Rule #2: Inspect What You Expect

If you can research your staff's performance prior to taking over the team, DO IT. If you can speak with a previous Supervisor prior to making a decision, DO IT. You never want to give away your dirty laundry and you never want to take someone else' dirty laundry.

Day 1, set your expectations with your team and address the issues that are high profile. Create an agenda. You may want to address some of the following points, while adding points you feel are important as well:

- *Morale*
- *Meetings expectations*
- *Special Projects*
- *Keep it professional*
- *Meal violations – what does that mean and why is it important*
- *Contests are equally unequal and not everyone gets to play*
- *Tracking accurate work time*
- *Exception time tracking*

- *Client detail tracking*
- *Attendance*
- *Call in sick policy*
- *Working hours*
- *Professionalism*
- *Dress Code*
- *Addressing frustrated clients*
- *Company Mission and core values*
- *Work flow*
- *Risks to clients*
- *Don't get fired over a nickel*
- *Productivity…what to expect*
- *What to do if systems go down*
- *How to cheat the system. Now that you know I know you know how to cheat the system – Don't!*
- *Reports*
- *My management styles*
- *What you can expect from me*
- *What you cannot expect from me*
- *Free Coaching*
- *You'll know exactly where you stand with me and your performance and know what's around the corner well in advance*

- *Meetings – Start on time, end on time, are general rather than specific and are structured*

Once you have covered the important things, it's time to stick to your commitments. You need to be on top of your game all the time. Your team looks up to you – or at least they should!

Prepare for your meeting by setting your agenda, having copies of material available, set an appointment for the team meeting with a room reserved and stick to your timeline. If it's an hour meeting, it's an hour meeting or less.

My first team meeting usually is a fun one around team building. It's a simple game and lasts about an hour. Here's how it goes. I buy two kids puzzles. One is a simple one and one is a bit harder. After mixing the two together, I separate the pieces out so that each person in the meeting gets about the same number of pieces. I place them in a baggy and place the boxes with the pictures in a hidden place (there's a reason for this).

Next, I assemble the troops in the room and have small talk for a couple of minutes while the stragglers come in. It's a good time to socialize and find out what's going on, how everyone is feeling and who's doing anything fun for the weekend. Once we are ready to officially get down to business, I start off with meeting ground rules. "O.k., I like to have fun and want our meetings to be fun. As we have our meetings, we will talk about the mass and not the one off's. In other words, if we are talking about workflow, I'm talking about workflow in general and not the 'I had this one client that [fill in with whatever obscure thing you want]'. I'm going to stop you and remind you that we are talking about big picture, o.k.?

I also what to talk about something that is important to me. Open discussion. In our team meetings, we will have open discussion. This is not a one-way communication. I want to hear what your thoughts are. It is o.k. to disagree with anything. How you disagree and how hard you disagree is a whole other story. You can politely ask for clarification or talk about why something doesn't make sense to you. That's it. I'll do what I can to explain a decision or take the feedback and put it in the parking lot so I can gnaw on it or decide you're right. I do not expect to hash things over a dozen times in a group meeting. If it is a change in something, I ask that you embrace it, even if you don't agree with it. Give it a chance. We can always go back and change things again, but we can't if you don't follow the change or find a work around that suits you. Oh, and please speak for yourself and not the group. One thing I hate is, 'Bryan, it's not just me, but everyone thinks [again, fill in the blank]."

Many times, one associate will be the negative associate and challenge you in the meeting. That's o.k. if it is respectful and there is a time when the discussion is over…or needs to be. Remember, you are the boss, and you are leading the group. Don't let it get out of control. From time to time, I have had to squash this behavior. I can recall a time when a behavior to show empathy on a return call was a requirement. One associate did not agree with this and so I explained the reasons behind it. Body language and history played a part in this conversation. I remember ending the conversation with, "You may not agree with me, but that is the final decision. End of discussion. If you'd like to discuss this further, we can after the meeting."

It was a harsh stance to take but it worked. In this instance, the associate realized my position and stopped challenging. She did not seek me out after the meeting, but I made a point to immediately pull her in to a room and discuss what happened. Again, it is o.k. to challenge but at a certain point it stops, or the entire meeting goes sideways and you as a leader loose respect from your group.

A little while later in the day another associate pulled me aside and said, "Bryan, thank you for taking control of the meeting. We're just not used to that kind of behavior, and we all saw you take action after the meeting."

Even though it wasn't spoken about what happened behind closed doors, the rest of the floor saw that it was being addressed. This is often missed in companies.

Sorry for the tangent. Now back to the original meeting:

"I noticed a couple of you straggled in a few minutes late to the meeting. Not looking for explanation why. No worries. I do want to set the expectation that when a meeting is called, I'd like to ensure everyone is here on time.

Finally, I expect your attention in the meeting. I do not expect to have side bar conversations or everyone talking at once. If it happens, expect to be called out. What do you guys think about that?"

Usually at this point there should be a little light joking if you're building rapport with the team. It may be a little too soon but by the end of the meeting everyone should feel a sense of bonding.

Now comes the fun part. I give everyone in the room a bag of the puzzle pieces. "Now we are going to see who the most analytical and fastest person in the room is. When I say 'go', you can start putting your puzzle pieces together. You can ask me for anything except for help putting your puzzle together. Ready? Set? GO!"

Your job as the leader is to watch and observe. There will be silence in the room. After a couple of minutes someone will say, "I can't find any that are fitting. Are you sure these are all mine?" I usually start to chuckle a bit. "Oh, sorry. John and Suzanne, you two get to work together. Bryan and Jeff, you start working together. Sorry." Observe the interaction and the conversation now that is taking place. After a few minutes, start pairing groups with groups and continue this until you have two groups of associates.

Look at who is directing the group. Listen to see who is frustrated with the project. Who is the cheerleader. Who is just sitting and watching. As things start to progress with the puzzles, someone will say, "Hey, I think we can use all the pieces". Don't combine the groups. Just acknowledge they are correct. At some point someone should say that they wish they could see the picture. I'll ask them if they needed anything. When they reply that they want a picture, I'll get their picture for them and say, "I told you I'm here and will answer anything you need except for putting the puzzle together."

Inevitably, one team will finally win, and someone will yell," WE DID IT. WE WIN". I'll reply, "Really? Everyone stop now. Let's talk about what just happened and who won?"

What you have just done is establish who has what strengths in your group, who needs development, who is the negative one, who is flying under the radar, who is the person for the rewards and recognition group, who is the strategizer, who is the leader, who is the analytical one, who is the jokester, who are best friends, etc.

I'll recap my observations and we will talk about the points. It should be pretty close to this:

- *At first, everyone was quiet and working by themselves*
- *When they started working in pairs, they started talking*
- *When they started working in groups, the groups started talking*
- *One or two people will generally step up to giving directions, one or two people will be the workers, a couple will sit back and*

watch, and a couple will look confused like they were looking for directions.

- *One person will ask for the picture*
- *Another person will follow and ask for the other picture*
- *One person will ask questions on behalf of the group*
- *When one group finishes they will cheer and high five and the other group will throw their hands up in defeat.*

Rule # 3: One Team – One Goal

Part of this exercise is the lesson that everyone lost because both puzzles were not completed. We are one team. As a company, we are one team. As a piece of the company, we are a contributing group to the overall team. We must interact well as a team but think outside the box and leverage the help of other teams in the division as well as other areas in the company such as training department, IT, Customer Service, Collections, Quality Assurance, Closing, etc.

Use Your Staff

After I left my last job, I was asked to help create an outbound call center for returning calls to clients. I'd do this as a contractor. I was up for the challenge and couldn't wait to put my Sig Sigma training back to use!

First, I needed to be trained on the process and work flow currently in effect. On arriving at the job, I found that the only training that was available was by sitting side by side with someone and learning the flow. I did this with several people. What I found is that everyone did it a different way and there were huge gaps in the process.

I decided I needed to create a training class for my new group. I did (which I'll talk about training in a different book.) At the same time I documented my new process, put it on a white board to find my holes and filled them, I interviewed potential associates and hired those that looked like a good fit.

It is important to remember, when hiring someone, do not just take their work history and title as gospel. If I have a person who is excellent in a particular job function but has an attitude or morale problem and I have another candidate who is a go getter, great morale, team player but doesn't know the business, I will take the second person every day. I can teach them what they need to know about the business. Low morale will kill a business.

I heard that people who are engaged and enjoy their job tend to come to work more often and are more productive. This makes sense to me. Isn't this where you spend most of your time away from home? Wouldn't YOU want to call in sick if you knew you were going to head off to a boring job where top-down management doesn't allow you to participate in a better working company?

Remember my first Supervisor at the last company I told you about, Kim? Well, one day, out of the blue, she gave me a call. We chatted for a while, I told her what I was doing, and she asked to come on board. I was delighted. I knew her caliber of work and work ethics.

After a very short period of time, the company recognized her abilities and asked her to come on board. She did. About that time, I decided that the company was a pretty great company and I wanted to jump on board as a permanent associate.

After making my intentions known to the Vice President, once again I was told that I was overqualified and he didn't think he could afford me. Once again, I explained the importance of having the opportunity for growth within a company and I liked a lot of things this company was doing.

Shortly after this, I was extended an offer with the conditional phrasing, "Bryan, this is the highest pay for this position. Anything higher is out of this pay scale." Incidentally, this was the lowest amount that my wife and I agreed to accept, so it worked out perfectly! I was now one of four managers for the Division. Kim and I were working together again, and we took the division by storm.

Kim began building relationships with everyone as did I. I created structured training and retrained the entire division. We were also experiencing a growth spurt in the division so I had to hire and train another hundred people over a 2 ½ month period of time. Kim and I made changes to processes, systems, and culture. It was whispered about that this was the Kim and Bryan show. That didn't bother me because it was good. The company was solid, just needed some new blood. Change for the better. Action instead of reaction.

I remember asking the Managers many questions around workflow and processes. Why do we do this process this way? Why do we ask this question? What values are added by completing these screens? Why does the system flow this way?

Every time I asked these questions, I got the same answer. "Because that's how it's been done for decades." This is not an acceptable answer to me. And it should never be an acceptable answer to you either. If you're not changing things, you're not improving.

Now, I'm not suggesting you challenge everything. It's good to ask questions and then form your line of attack. What is the low hanging fruit? What makes the most sense to challenge first and change? What is worth fighting for? (In every instance, your associates are worth fighting for).

I decided to make a few changes and one of the Managers came up to me and said, "You can't do that." His concern was that it was not approved! I gave him Management 101 which includes doing things outside the scope of your job. It's o.k. to change things if you keep everyone in the loop. I had already discussed some of the changes I wanted to implement with the Sr. V.P and the CEO and was given no push back not to. "Sounds good, Bryan. Keep me in the loop." I did and the changes were well accepted by the associates.

One day the Sr. V.P. called me in his office. "Bryan, I have an idea. It's really rough, but I want to create a new department." He went on to tell me his high-level thoughts of a hybrid department with the vision that would later become the standard protocol for one of the current Divisions once it was flushed out and piloted. Then he asked if I was up to the challenge. Of course, I was excited and said yes. He wanted the plans ready to go…in under a week. I let him know that two weeks was more realistic. He agreed and said, "Put it together, Bryan. If anyone here can, it's you. Use duct tape if you need to. By the way, you'll be reporting in directly to me."

Sure enough, two weeks later we took our first call. It was a success…and used a LOT of duct tape. Over the next nine months the workflows and processes were refined, I began managing this department and co managed another department with a different skill set. The reward for the hard work? Winner of the President's Club with an all-expense paid seven-day cruise with the executive team and a week's additional vacation plus paid vacation for the cruise, Manager of the year with a little bonus and another paid day off…and that was just the beginning. Oh, while on the cruise I even went Ziplining in Mexico, my wife and I were received a spa day on the ship (courtesy of the CEO) and the ability to relate to and interact with the Executive team, off the clock, if you will.

For my annual review, my Sr. V.P scheduled lunch with me at a very nice restaurant. Before we got to the review itself, he let me know that "Meets Expectations" means I am doing my job right. He said he was a rather tough grader. We then went over the actual review. There were an awful lot of Exceeds Expectations. I was pleased that I made the right decision to join this great company. Oh, this Sr. V.P. has the culture I was used to and worked so hard to instill in my new job with this company. Although I didn't know it at the time, he too worked at the same company Kim, and I worked at together.

A new Sr. Manager was hired to help manage the other division and make it grow. We got along great and spent a lot of time together and we would toss ideas off each other. Crazy ideas. We made some major changes to processes and workflows. We leveraged the resources and workflows from other departments to boost our departments. It was great! Oh, this Sr. Manager? Although I didn't know it at the time, he too worked at the same company Kim and I worked at together.

Not too much later in the year, word was announced that the company had won a multibillion-dollar contract. A new sister company needed to be built and that Sr. V.P. I was telling you about? He was the architect behind it and became the President of this new company. He pulled that Sr. Manager I was telling you about over to become the Director of the new company, who in turn pulled me over to build one of the Divisions.

Not quite confident in building the new company, I spent some time with my old Sr. V.P. and with my CEO. We discussed the options. Both of them supported whatever decision I would make, with my Sr. V.P. digging at me. "Bryan, I don't know. You could stay here or build something new! President's Club, Manager of the year…Sounds like a pattern here." Incidentally, I did make the jump and a few months later, there it was. The new company had their annual gathering with all Associates. Although there was not a President's Club or Manager of the year award established yet (the company was just starting up), there was generally the highest award – the Rock Star award. Yep. It went to me and a select few that really were Rock Stars.

The new Director started from scratch and wanted to build the culture of the new company to somewhat mirror the culture of the company we both learned so much from years ago.

Many of the Senior staff that joined the new company, well, guess what. Many worked at the same company Kim and I worked at. Many I knew and worked with while others I did not know but had heard of. We all clicked immediately. Even the people that never worked at my earlier company had the right skill set, attitude and enthusiasm. We began putting our different divisions together like we had worked with each other for years already.

My division had high visibility. It had to be perfect. I had a great bunch of peers to help me do it.

We were so in tune with each other that we could finish the other's thoughts. For those that had not worked in our previous environment before but had been asked to join the team, it was quite a shock, but we all meshed extremely well. Great interviewing and great references built a stellar team. Our new visionary thinking went into action and we started getting things done, watched each other's back, had fun and built a well implemented process very quickly. If something didn't work right, we changed it. We stress tested the division before we went live. We learned a lot. Kept a 'lessons learned log' and an 'issues log'. Both essential for future changes. More stuff to teach you in another book.

Many of us sat in a room with the administrators of the programs we were going to run and participated in the many JAD sessions (Joint Application Development sessions). There was a lot of talent in the room and this multibillion-dollar venture hit the ground running.

Remember Jeff? One day I received an email from him which said he was moving into town and was looking for a job. Guess where he works now? Yep. With me again.

Rule #4: Give it your best

Believe it or not, your team knows what you are doing at any level. They know what you are not doing as well. If you have issues at home, leave them there. Come to work and give your team which is your extended family your full attention. If you do not allow your Associates to do something in the office such as eat at their desk or use their cell phones, then you shouldn't either. Your team will respect you and will work better as a team.

I have seen so many teams fall apart as a result of poor leadership.

Start your shift when you are supposed to as well. There's nothing like requiring members of a team to arrive to work on time only to find their leader is consistently late or leaving early. Put yourself out there. Give it your all. As a leader, you have the ability (with the right company) to take a day off or leave early or come in late without penalty. That's not the point I'm making. It is the leader that always – every day – comes in late, leaves early, doesn't give development feedback, doesn't answer questions, makes personal calls, disagrees with "management", and basically is your bottom feeder leader that causes low morale.

I recall having a conversation with one Associate that I had recently taken on just two days earlier. She came from a dysfunctional team. I asked what didn't work on her last team. She let me know…first thing out of her mouth without hesitation, (Paraphrased) [The leader] didn't lead. If there was a question, he said to go ask so and so. People would come to work late, call in sick. It was horrible. It was a standing joke with the team that they could do whatever they wanted and that's what the problem was. Everyone was trying to push him to the limit to see how far they could go. She said that she was guilty of it too.

Rule #5:
Establish Strong Relationships With the Right People

When you are the real deal, your reputation speaks for itself. Build a relationship with your boss and don't stop there. Build good relationships with all leaders all the way up to the CEO. The stronger your reputation for getting things done, the right way, the more freedom you will have to do things on your own. Building a strong relationship with other departments is more than just hanging out talking about what's going on over the weekend or the latest sports.

Take the time to give unsolicited positive feedback and recognition to Associates in other departments. It doesn't mean you need to CC the individual you are complimenting. Instead, send the compliment to his boss. Let his boss give the praise. Work well done deserves recognition and builds on relationships with other departments.

A great example of this is IT. When is the last time IT was recognized for a job well done. I actually think the work that IT does is amazing with the right group of people. More often than not, there is a complaint email when something breaks, a ticket isn't completed on time, a change is made behind the scenes and operations isn't aware of the change in advance, etc. It's a thankless job.

My suggestion? Take the thankless part and turn it in to a thank you. It will be worth it. This leads me in to our next subject.

Trust Your Team. Use Your Team. Develop Your Team.

Your team must trust you and trust you can lead them and make the best decisions for them. Many leaders believe they have the best ideas and the best way to run things. This simply isn't true. People that report in to you are closer to the front line than you are. Going all the way down to the front line workers and getting their input on a new change, policy, procedure is key. If you want to refine your process, it is best if you take a small team of 5-8 front line workers and put them in the room. Explain the dilemma that you are facing and ask them to come up with some ideas on how to attack it. For example, you hear through the grapevine that the workflow is too long and out of order from reality. The associates are really getting down and it is affecting the morale on the floor.

Here's a situation:
Being a wise leader (and you can do this at any level) you decide to go to the floor and talk to

your workers (you should be sure to visit your floors and see how things are going at least 3 times a week if you are in Sr. Management). During your visit, you are chit chatting with one of your Leaders. In the conversation you discover that some associates think the workflow is out of order and could be changed so that client's experience is better.

Because you are a wise leader, you look at the workflow and make a bunch of changes that you think are the right changes to make and roll it out to the division! Problem solved, right? WRONG! There is a big uproar on the floor. The Associates are talking, "This new workflow is stupid!" "I liked the old way better." "The other system was so much faster."

What happened? You made the changes.

Try this. Same source of discovering the issue. Instead of solving the problem yourself, you decide to get a focus group of 5 working associates in a room. To do this you decide to talk to your managers in your next team meeting. "Team, when I was on the floor the other day, I was told that the workflow was out *of whack and there may be a way to make the client's experience a lot better. What do you think?" Now, your managers are going to tell you what's on their mind. If you have a perfect team, all will give you honest feedback, but most likely you have something like this…Some will agree and give you their ideas of how the workflow should be changed. Some will be silent and some will say it works just fine. The associates are just complainers!*

Thank them for their opinions. "I am going to meet with some of the associates and see what their ideas are. I'll send an appointment out to them for a strategy meeting. MaLisa, would you like to take the lead on this? You said you wanted to develop your leadership skills more. This would be a perfect opportunity." MaLisa is a little hesitant so you reassure her you will walk her through the process this time.

The next day you meet with the associates that were chosen. You were smart though. You chose three positive associates, an associate that is usually quiet and one of your outspoken or slightly resistant associates. Why did you choose this particular group of associates?

Because you wanted the positive people to help guide the right direction for the new workflow and your outspoken associate was chosen because of just that. He is outspoken. He is a huge benefit to the process. If anyone is going to talk about what's wrong, it's him. With that you will have a good group to prepare the presentation. Here is the big win though. When the group is finished with presentation of what needs to change in the workflow, they will give it to you. Most likely it will be along the lines of what you would change. There will also be some recommendations that you do not agree with. Your final version you can tweak it (this will be after you ask them some leading questions that will result in the group saying, "Yes, that doesn't make sense. Let's remove it or change that piece.")

The real value added to the group?

> *MaLisa gets developed and learns to lead a small group. MaLisa doesn't need to be in the group's meetings all the time and when she is, it should be to observe how the group is interacting and be there for when the group goes off task or cannot*

come to a united decision. MaLisa will be happy because she is refining a new skill set. Keep in mind, you may need to lead the first few group sessions so MaLisa can see how to keep the group together without fighting and so she can see when it is time to jump in and when it is time to sit back and observe. Healthy debate is a good thing. Arguing is not good.

➢ *The group gets to learn how to think through a process (you of course have taught them in the opening meetings what the expectations are, the end goal, what is in scope, what is out of scope, communication expectations, deadline and how to white board the process). You'll also have to teach them over time how to give you updates. MaLisa too. Bullet points. I like the rule that if it is more than three bullet points, it's too long. You get the point. Now for data, you'll want them to have a minimum of 6 reference points over time. This establishes there is a trend, and this is what it is.*

> ➤ *The group is a good group of associates, and they deserve time away from normal daily duties. Reward your performers.*

> ➤ *The biggest win for this is that when it is done, guess who is going to roll it out to the rest of the division and train the rest of the division? Yes, the training department most likely, but the training department will have this group of associates in each training class. They, the people who built it, not "management". They get to explain why the changes are what they are. They get to take the credit and the hits.*

> ➤ *The group gets the credit. You get the credit because the group reports to you.*

> ➤ *The group is engaged.*

> ➤ *Everyone wants to be in the group so productivity goes up along with morale!*

Now imagine having 5 or 6 of these groups working on different things. Different special projects. You are now MANAGING. Guess what! That's what you are paid to do.

If your team can do their job in your absence, this is a big win.

Now, keep in mind, when you reward people and give special projects, think about the skill set and who you are choosing. Don't pick the same people all the time. Don't pick the people that have strength in a particular area every time. You want to grow your people not just utilize their strength. Most important, choose different teams, nationalities, sexes, etc.

Remember, nonperformers are going to gossip about how it is not fair, point out when your performers mess up every time and, well, gossip! YOU need to nip this in the butt.

When it comes to contests or incentives, all need to understand that it is equally unequal. Not everyone can play and not everyone playing will play fair. It's a bonus above the day to day pay. Some may cheat but you, being the great leader you are, will look at the top 10% for potential cheaters. This is where you find out great ways to improve processes. Why are they in the top 10% or are they cheating. Again, inspect what you expect.

MISCILANIOUS STUFF

If the nonperformers are not on your team and you cannot directly change behavior and their leader cannot change their behavior or refuses to address, you need to have your team continue to adapt. When your team asks "How come we have to change? Why do we have to work Saturdays? Why do we have to adjust our schedules and they don't?"

If you are a great leader, you will remind them to focus on their job and that all things generally work out. You know this because of the diligence you have put in keeping track of your conversations and events that have occurred. You have built your foundation for your argument to change [insert whatever needs change that is out of your control].

Your log of everything you have done will soon come out because your team is focused and doing the right behaviors. The biggest complainers are generally the nonperformers. Sooner or later a great leader will manage them out or they will be so unhappy they leave. That's o.k., protect your performers.

Meetings

➤ Meetings are important. There are three types of meetings. #1 Team Meetings - where you are giving information and changes or updates.

➤ #2 Presentation Meetings – You and your team are presenting a new idea, change, audit results, etc.

➤ #3 Meetings with potentially hostile, or outside decision makers.

➤ (There is a fourth but we will delve in to that in another book – Skip Level meetings).

#1 Team Meetings:

This type of meeting should occur with your staff at least twice a month or as needed to cover several things. Quality is important so have a meeting that revolves around work *performance or trending. These meeting are where you cover recent updates, policy changes, upcoming changes. You will discuss what is or is not working correctly from the Associate's perspective as well. Remember, this is not a time for vocal Associate to vent. It's where constructive discussion around areas of opportunity should happen.*

You should have a meeting on process/flow improvement and Quality. These meetings should be interactive, and you should have a group discussion with your input being the last. Ask leading questions. Listen to what is being said in the meeting by others first. The great thing about this is that everyone has an opinion, and the opinion may not be yours. Let them get their arguments out on the table first. Study what they are saying. This gives you the greatest upper hand. Why do you think that is? Because you know their arguments and stance. Now you get to give your input. There may be great ideas on the table that you will need to take away and research or implement. On the other hand, there may be reasons for why 'it is what it is'. Rather than try to talk to points that may be irrelevant to their concerns, you know specifically what their issues are, and you can address their specific concerns. It also gives your Associates the sense that you care, and you are listening. It's perfect!

If you are meeting with associates, don't just read stuff! Know your material in advance and give the handouts but then talk about the general overview of the handouts. You are on stage. You must be upbeat and the center of attention. Don't just give the answers! Involve the group in the discussions. Have them talk through processes. Make them think.

Be sure to call on the person for input that is not engaged, is doing something else like doodling or looks like they are bored with the whole thing.

For team meetings, set your agenda. For an hour long meeting, I like to have 3 major components which lasts 15 minutes each at max. The last 15 minutes should be for open discussion about anything else that is going on or that needs to be on the table.

In order to keep a meeting on track with healthy discussion, there are often times that you will need to cut the discussion off and table it for later. That means that we are done with this right now.

If you have action items given to you in a meeting from your team that you agree to follow up on, do it. Do it quickly and don't wait for the next meeting. Recap all meetings and send it out to the participants within 24 hours following the meeting. <u>Always send a recap memo out.</u> It is better to say, "Well, Joel, that's a great question. Let me put it in the parking lot and I'll get back to you. Much better than trying to b.s. your way through an answer. Here's an example of a question raised in a meeting which was put in the parking lot (something that you needed to research):

"Team, as we discussed you questioned why we ask the client if we can call them by their first name. Here is what I've found out. Some cultures do not like being called by their first name and some professions do not as well. As a result, we will continue to ask this question and comply with what the client replies with. It will give us a better client experience."

#2: Presentation meetings:

You are presenting a presentation to your boss. In this meeting you want to set up the presentation.

> *Have a clear and bulleted PowerPoint overhead presentation ready.*

> *Check the room by reserving it for an extended period of time.*

> *Make sure everything works.*

> *Strategically place where your audience will sit as well as you and your presenters.*

> *Have your presenters handy to explain and get them to participate in the presentation.*

> *It's not all about you. If they did the leg work, let them present. Be sure they are ready and have their support documentation on hand. You may want to do several dry runs in advance.*

➢ *If you have projections or timelines, give yourself some padding. Things change.*

➢ *Better to under promise than over promise. I like to pad my numbers when I can by about 20%. Depends on what I'm selling.*

➢ *Be on time. Have coffee or some beverage available.*

➢ *Rehearse your presentation with your group. You want a solid presentation. Ask questions of the group that you can anticipate will be asked in the meeting.*

➢ *If you are given follow up tasks after the presentation, be sure to give a timeline that is realistic and not to aggressive.*

➢ *Double check your data*

➢ *Create a professional PowerPoint for the presentation and practice. Be animated and don't just read the PowerPoint! Summarize the slides.*

#3: Meetings with Outside Sources:

Anytime you have a meeting with someone that can impact you or your operation, you must proceed with caution. Make sure your statements are formed correctly. Errors that are pointed out can be fatal. I have been in too many of these meetings where a peer will point out some dirty laundry or make a statement about something not working across the board which is not accurate. These are immediately escalated (even if it is not reacted to in the meeting by the other party), generally there will be questions down the road – like right after the meeting. Remain professional.

There are so many other things to talk about when it comes to Meetings, so we'll address that in another publication.

Management Says

I can't tell you how many times I have heard Team Leaders, Supervisors and Managers say to their people, "Well, we have to do it this way because Upper Management Says So!" or "Upper Management changed [input change here]".

<u>*If you don't buy it, you can't sell it!*</u>

If you are rolling something out that is a change or new to the process, you best believe in it. Argue behind closed doors but when the doors open, YOU are management. You had better sell it. "Because I said so" is also another reason that should never be used. People like specifics. They need to buy in to things. If you don't believe it, they won't believe it and things will fall apart quickly. Blaming UP always backfires.

This is the biggest reasons I see disconnect between workers and management. Usually, the leader that doesn't have the buy-in is the leader that is the least effective with the team that doesn't buy in to the change, has the most negative attitudes and lowest performance.

Development – U and I

I am constantly asked what is a U and I?

This is where YOU get to talk, and I get to listen. It is 30 minutes to an hour of you talking about whatever you want. Could be your life, the team, what you're involved in, what's working and what is not working. It's not time to talk about coaching, stats, performance, etc. This will generally give you insight to a lot with the person. It will tell you what they are interested in and what they want to do. You can use this to leverage their strengths and desires. It will also help you manage the person.

It might be possible there was a recent death in the family. This might explain a change in a performer that is now under performing. Most companies have an EAP (Employee Assistance Program) where they can get free services, legal and emotional. Perhaps there is a divorce going on or a spouse that was just put in jail. It's been so helpful to have these U&I's over the years.   Minimum once a quarter.   This is different from coaching sessions.

Coaching and Developing

Coaching sessions are for developmental purposes. I don't believe in hiding the bottom 10%. You are where you are. If you have a strong team, your team will rally to get the bottom performers to the top. Have conversations with your associates once a month on their performance. If they can hear their call or view some data so they can see where to improve, give it to them.

Give them the option to improve. You don't have to babysit them or ensure they follow your development plan; you just need to offer it to them. One of the things I rarely do is give the answer to something someone has already been taught. If I do, guess what. I'm going to be asked a question every five minutes and will be expected to give the answer – over and over and over. I want my team to think. I'll ask probing questions until they uncover the answer. You have to let your team know why you are asking the probing questions in advance until they understand your management style.

Walk your floor. Spend time with your Associates. I guarantee if you walk your floor and listen/observe, you will hear where your Associates are fumbling and be able to give immediate feedback or assistance.

Look at your reports and analyze your top 10% and bottom 10%. Look at your top 10% and see if there is cheating. If the Associate is cheating the system to achieve high numbers, that could cause a huge risk to your company. You also may be able to find super star performers and be able to ask them for tips on what they are doing to achieve their results. This is good stuff to share with the rest of your staff. It will help get the next group of performers up just a notch.

Look at your bottom 10% as well. What is going on? Do they need additional tools to increase performance? Too often leaders will just cut someone without advance notice for performance. Not good. Give constant feedback. Everyone deserves to know exactly what is around the corner. If you miss a step of discipline, don't surprise the Associate with a Final Written Warning. Take it on your shoulders and back up. They absolutely deserve to know what their next step is.

Most importantly in a one-on-one coaching session do not overwhelm them. Give them the 3 biggest low hanging fruits they can fix in their performance. Once they have fixed those, go after the next ones. Trying to fix performance by telling the person <u>everything</u> they need to fix is not productive and overwhelming. Acknowledge improvements.

Always document your time with your staff and inspect what you expect. In the past I have asked my associates to give me a sample of what they think their best work is for the day. The reason to do this is because they think they are giving perfect work to you. This allows you to really know who needs additional training or assistance. When you correct their mistakes, it addresses exactly what they need to address. Continue this a few times until you get what you are looking for. Once this is accomplished, you can let the group know that now you will be doing random audits now.

Constant feedback is critical. Associates need to know where they are in performance and be allowed free coaching. That part is all fun. When it comes to discipline and write-ups which can lead to termination, they need to know what's around the corner. That's a whole different book. But I'll give you an example of what has happened time and time again.

Attendance. Pretty important. As a patter develops, I'll bring it up to the associate. As time progresses, I'll bring them in to my office and discuss the problem. I'll ask what I can do to assist and remind them that attendance is in their control. I'll let them know they're getting a Verbal Written notice. This will be stern but casual conversation.

Next time they're out, boom. First Written warning. Don't miss a beat. This is not such a nice meeting with them my voice and expressions will be more specific.

Next time they're out, BOOM. Second Written warning. This time I express the conversations we have had and that it is going to cost them their job if it continues.

Next time they're out, BOOM BOOM. My body language, posture and word choice as well as expressions are stern. Very stern. This is the end of the rope. I'll ask them what they think will happen next. They'll say another write up most likely. I'll reply, "Nope. I've given you every opportunity to change your behavior. I've explained how it impacts the morale on the floor, how I staff to expected numbers based on volumes. This is the last warning."

3 of 5 times, the Associate will resign to avoid the termination. It also saves me time from having to terminate someone for cause, have them file for unemployment and having to go down for a hearing to fight the appeal.

Quality Assurance

Many companies have a Quality Assurance department. This is different from a Quality Control Department. The QA department is the department that independently monitors an associate's performance by reviewing areas of work or recordings to ensure policy and procedure are being followed. It is important for a leader to partner with the QA department and it is more so important that an upper management person ensures they keep a pulse on the QA department. The QA department should have set things that they deduct for, however not everything is black and white. There needs to be an escalation process and timeline as well as the opportunity for the associate to hear their call or see their scores and deductions in a timely manner.

Although the QA department must have their own leader, the QA department must run based on the operations guidelines and not that of what the QA department implements. There should be a definitions document stating what each section holds and there must be an ability to challenge that score on several levels with the final decision being made between the operations head and the QA head. Do what is right for the company and for the associate.

Although there is a QA department, the Team Leader, Supervisor and Manager should randomly listen to calls periodically. Supervisors and Managers should randomly sample calls. This is easy to do while you are typing up documents, reviewing performance and creating presentations. You are looking for the overall behavior of the call. Team Leaders should perform this function on every associate. Depending on how long each workflow is, this may be one to five times a month. It should be documented, like all things, and reviewed with the associate.

For calls that are QA'd by Quality Assurance, the leader must review the call first and either agree with the scoring or challenge the score. If the associate challenges the score, the leader will need to be able to logically explain why the score is accurate. Otherwise, the leader and QA are not on the same page. Without this QA will become the bad guy. With this, they are the good guy. Always accurate. It makes it much easier when the leader and QA can talk through things prior to giving feedback to the associate. It makes for a great relationship.

An "Auto Zero" or Fatal Error is a serious risk to the company. The Associate had done something that puts or could put the company at risk. Ultimately, repeated fatal errors will result in the termination of employment. Immediately listen to the call or review the process for the error and give immediate feedback to the Associate. Document your conversation. Have the Associate review the process or listen to the call. Do NOT let the Associate know that it's no big deal. If it's a fail, it's a fail. Once feedback is given and an action plan is set to prevent this in the future, document the plan, send a copy to QA and follow up with the Associate frequently on their progress.

Will or Skill

In a job when someone is failing, it is either will or skill. They have the will but don't have the training to do the job properly or they have been coached and developed and just don't want to do the job. If it is will, you will want to manage them out quickly. You don't need the negativity on the floor. Everyone is paid 100% of the time. You ask for 80% efficiency. It is not fair to you or your workers to have someone cheat the system.

On the flip side, some people just are not a fit for the job. In either case, the associate has a clear path of where they are going and what is around the corner if you constantly talk to them and don't sugar coat it.

Keep good documentation and a game plan in mind when working with someone not interested in working. You will need this to present to HR.

Final Thoughts

There are many areas of management that must be addressed but are frequently overlooked. This book covers some of the basic leadership skills and best practices that are often missed or not taught. This is the low hanging fruit. The basics. This book can be a great book for the person who has never lead a team yet but seeks to. Other topics for discussion are Training, meeting goals and deadlines, development, discipline from beginning to termination, efficiency improvement, user acceptance testing, JAD sessions, project management, presentation, both written and verbal and many other topics I look forward to giving you the opportunity to read.

It is my wish that you will take from this book the general context of what is here and use what is important to you. I hope that your Associates feel like a part of your team, and I hope that this spreads like wildfire.

One thing that is priceless is getting feedback from my Associates and giving surveys to find out product and process knowledge. I'd like to do this with you as well. Will you please take a couple of minutes and visit http://www.surveymonkey.com/s/CXGB7RL where I have created a survey. I'd very much appreciate your feedback, suggestions, and testimonials.

Bryan L. Hartson, Sr.

About the Author

Bryan Hartson, *at the time of this writing, is a 56-year young person, Sig Sigma Yellow Belt and NFCCC Certified, who has a strong belief that because one spends a majority of their time at work, work should be a place to make a difference and that teams should be cohesive, self sufficient and opinions do count – Actually they make a difference.*

In his early years, Bryan decided to seek his education as quickly as possible and enter Chiropractic College. In doing so he solicited the assistance of the Dean of his college, Fullerton College, to take 42 semester units in one semester. His Dean stated that this could not be done, but if he wanted to, he could write a letter of explanation which would have to be approved by two Deans of the college. Bryan created his compelling letter and returned it the same day. Shortly thereafter, Bryan was granted the ability to follow his dream. Bryan was determined and received high marks in his coursework at the college. He completed one of his final exams from his hospital bed.

Bryan is a cancer survivor as are both of his daughters, Kaitlynn and Ashley, 24 and 25 respectfully. His 15 year old son, Bryan Jr., carries the gene and will be undergoing his treatment in a few years. The disease is FAP (Familial Adenomas Polyposis) which manifests thousands of polyps in the large intestine requiring the complete removal of the colon or certain death would occur.

It is the true desire to spread techniques in management that improve not only the lives of the Associates, but that as well of the lives of those the product for the company serve. In doing this, the mission of making a difference in the world one life at a time is served. A positive work life transitions into coming home to a happy, balanced home life.

Bryan was the Senior Call Center Manager for the third largest Non-Prime mortgage company in the Nation and has managed from inception a call center focused on keeping families in their home during or following financial crisis or *assist homeowners in transitioning out of their property with grace.*

Bryan welcomes feedback and comments at Bryan.Hartson@yahoo.com

Comments about Bryan L. Hartson, Sr.

As posted on Linkedin.com

- *"Bryan is a hard working, team-oriented manager who strives to make improvements to achieve operational goals. He is willing to do what it takes to get the job done with optimal results and with a positive, "can do" attitude." Dawn Elmore, VP Default Administration*

- *"Bryan did a great job in helping our business achieve and surpass our goals and objectives. He was very knowledgeable about his area and routinely looked for new ways to enhance the partnership between our two businesses." Joe Leskowski, VP*

- *"Upon joining Option One, I found Bryan to be one of the most technically proficient managers within operations. He has a keen ability to understand the details that most* managers at his level take for granted. Bryan's leadership style is fair, yet demanding. He expects his team to achieve superior results and is prepared to roll up his sleeves to accomplish the common goals. I fully endorse Bryan as a senior leader." Richard Gilmartin, Director

- "In my interactions with Bryan, he came across as an accomplished operational manager with an in depth understanding of the business process which he was managing. This along with his ability to understand data produced by processes and the ability to use data intelligently to manage an operation makes him a very valuable member of any organization." Amit Misar, Director, Servicing Systems

- "Bryan is a great strategist and overall manager. He has the ability to solve complex business problems and apply efficient solutions that deliver results. He has a strong collection and call center operations

background. I highly recommend him!"
Sonny Nguyen, Solicitation Manager

- *"Bryan is an excellent leader. He is always on top of his projects and is constantly looking for ways to improve productivity for the organization. I have witnessed him address large groups of associates. Brian commanded respect while effectively communicating with his people. He keeps the associates informed of the department goals and the opportunities for improvement while motivating them at the same time. Brian would be a fine addition to any team." Pat Stafford, AVP District manager*

- *"If you're looking for someone with energy, drive, creativity and performance, Bryan Hartson is the person for the job. I have worked very closely with Bryan over the past few years and found him to be a manager of outstanding caliber. He is highly skilled and extremely knowledgeable in the field of mortgage servicing. His excellent interpersonal skills and desire for excellence are key factors to his success."* Julia Langston, Sr. Operations Manager

- *"I worked closely with Bryan to achieve common goals at Option One. He was always upbeat, energetic and full of dynamic ideas. He is an intelligent and truly talented individual!"* Nancy Chappell, Call Center strategy Administrator

- *"Bryan is dependable, honest and easy to work with. He knows what he wants and is not afraid to go after it. I have worked with Bryan for 2 years now and I as a client he has been responsive, direct and consistent. I highly recommend Bryan Hartson."* Liga Svikes, Guest Services Manager

- *"Bryan and I had an opportunity to collaborate on a project together that helped bring our two divisions more in line with reaching a common goal. I found Bryan to be the consummate professional who was very attentive to the issues at hand, great with follow-up, a fantastic communicator, and a team player. Reaching our goal could not have been a success without the expertise and motivation that he brought to the group. I thoroughly enjoyed working with Bryan and am extremely confident in his leadership and project management abilities." Ed Van Duren, VP Production*

- *"Bryan is professional & knowledgeable in his position. I can always count on him to provide me with everything I need to ensure that both of our departments were being accommodated for all business needs involving both of our teams. Bryan is dedicated to his job & always a pleasure to work with.", Kim Martinez, QA Team Leader*

- *"I worked closely with Bryan for over a year on improving agent productivity for both Inbound and Outbound call center teams. I have worked with Operations Managers closely in many positions in the past but few have the dedication that I found with Bryan. He is committed to understanding the feedback even when negative and working to improve the business. He would respond very quickly with the right plan to improve the actionable item. I felt that we had a true partnership on making improvements which would directly impact the bottom line of the business. I have found that this type of interaction between Operations and Workforce teams difficult to achieve but it was easy to accomplish with Bryan. He was well liked by everyone he interacted with from agent to Senior Management even though the business was going through difficult times and he had to make some tough decisions. I highly recommend Bryan and believe he can succeed at any task assigned." David Mathieson, Performance Analyst Workforce Manager*

- *"I have worked closely with Bryan on an array of projects over the past year and he has come across as being highly skilled, excellent with people, and extremely motivated to get the job done right. He is always quick to establish real time solutions to problems using data driven analysis, which he is not scared to obtain himself. Bryan has been a positive influence in my career allowing me to learn, grow, and develop skills that will help me for years to come."* Parker Fayen, Reporting Specialist

- *"I worked with Bryan for a lengthy period of time while developing policies and procedures and participating in other projects for his department. His in-depth knowledge of the Collections processes and systems, prompt responses to inquiries, and hands-on management style were very refreshing. His friendly attitude and rapport with his subordinates, peers and superiors alike were well known and appreciated by all. I would not hesitate to recommend Bryan for a position with any organization."* Shantha Ramesh, Sr. P&P Writer

- *"I worked with Bryan for several years at Option One. Bryan is a hard-working, results-driven, detail-oriented leader who works well with people. I found him to be very candid, open to feedback, and always looking to improve. I enjoyed working with Bryan."* Steve Bartholomew, HR

- *"I have worked with Bryan for several years and have been impressed with his situational management style and ability to lead a large call center through good and challenging years. His ability to not only make difficult decisions and changes are complimented by his ability to bring divisional associate and management buy in. He listens to his associate's ideas and implements those that prove to be successful. Bryan is a great find and I highly recommend his talent."* Becky Paredes, Project Specialist

- *"My interactions with Bryan have always been enjoyable. He is well respected with his associates, peers and superiors. Bryan pays* attention to detail and thinks beyond the small scope of a project, process or operation to the bigger picture." Will Meeks, HR

- "Bryan is a conscientious, business minded leader. His ability to successfully balance his focus on both his subordinates as well as the business is apparent. I believe it is this balance that has continually made him successful within the Servicing organization." John Cruz, HR

- "I had the great pleasure to work with Bryan in process changes for quite some time. I'm impressed with his attention to detail, quick response and action and ability to lead change. He is personable, professional and very timely in his presentation and responses. His integrity is unsurpassable. A true professional and leader. Without fail, Bryan has been a constant in excellence and support to me and my team." Pritam Jain, CMT

- *"Bryan has been a great asset to our team. His strong strategically knowledge and dedication to doing whatever it takes to "get the job done" has been instrumental to the success of our team. He has the ability to find gaps in processes and apply effective solutions that deliver results. He is a pleasure to work with and has always remained a team player."* Mikel Machini, Customer Contact Service manager

- *"Bryan is a very passionate leader that always is looking to improve his and the departments performance. He is very analytical, detail-oriented, and because of this, he will find where we can improve ourselves. His dedication to his peers is what makes working with him such a pleasure. There is much you can learn from Bryan!"* David Ornelas, Project Manager

- *"I have the up most respect for Bryan Hartson. Bryan is my Sr. Operations Manager and it has been a pleasure working with and for him. Bryan has brought out qualities in me that I did not know I had. He knows how to bring out the best in his associates. Bryan has always made himself available to all associates and strongly believes in "open door" management policy. I have to contribute a majority of my success to the work environment Bryan has created at OOMC. Emilio Acuna, Loan Consultant*

NOTES

www.ingramcontent.com/pod-product-compliance
Lightning Source LLC
Chambersburg PA
CBHW051546170526
45165CB00002B/896